The Boat of Feelings

Quotes and Poems

VIBHA JAIN

NOTION PRESS

NOTION PRESS

India. Singapore. Malaysia.

This book has been published with all reasonable efforts taken to make the material error-free after the consent of the author. No part of this book shall be used, reproduced in any manner whatsoever without written permission from the author, except in the case of brief quotations embodied in critical articles and reviews.

The Author of this book is solely responsible and liable for its content including but not limited to the views, representations, descriptions, statements, information, opinions and references ["Content"]. The Content of this book shall not constitute or be construed or deemed to reflect the opinion or expression of the Publisher or Editor. Neither the Publisher nor Editor endorse or approve the Content of this book or guarantee the reliability, accuracy or completeness of the Content published herein and do not make any representations or warranties of any kind, express or implied, including but not limited to the implied warranties of merchantability, fitness for a particular purpose. The Publisher and Editor shall not be liable whatsoever for any errors, omissions, whether such errors or omissions result from negligence, accident, or any other cause or claims for loss or damages of any kind, including without limitation, indirect or consequential loss or damage arising out of use, inability to use, or about the reliability, accuracy or sufficiency of the information contained in this book.

QUOTES

Two beautiful hearts always

support each other.

Say goodbye to your past and give
your thanks to it for teaching you
some required lessons of life.

Some people use the silent treatment to control you, if possible, leave those people as this treatment hurts more than words.

Always be there for your loved one
and help them get back on the
correct track if they stray.

People who have time for others but
not for you, are not entitled to
your time either.

Cross your boundaries only when your heart allows you to do so, not when others want you to do so.

Sometimes times and circumstances take you away from people who don't deserve your love and affection so that better people can make room in your life.

Our pillow knows very
well the story behind our tears.

The battle between the heart and
the mind goes a little deeper on
the subject of love.

In the world of social media, if you
block, unfollow, or unfriend someone,
then there is nothing wrong with it
because your mental peace is more
important and should always
be your first priority.

"Sorry" is such a magic word, which when spoken at the right time can heal many broken relationships. Use it but only when you want to apologise to someone from the heart. Do not use it just for show.

People take those people for granted,

whom they have no fear

of losing.

We should start appreciating endings
when they are necessary for
better beginnings.

Sorry, please, thank you, how are you? are magical words that strengthen relationships. Don't be stingy about using these words.

15

Restriction is that sign board
that displays your personal
boundaries and cautions others
against stepping over them.

16

Don't lose your originality by going
along with the crowd.

Holding back your tears will just make you
feel heavier and worse; let them out.

There is no right time for doing your favourite things, you can do them anytime to make yourself happy.

Spend delightful moments with loved ones so that you can treasure them as lovely memories for the rest of your life.

Take hold of your loved one's hand

firmly and lovingly.

Embrace all of life's tiny moments and cherish them.

We are all humans. We make mistakes. So, never regret the mistake of trusting the wrong people, as these people help to clear our vision about the type of people we don't want in our lives.

Always be in the company of positive, inspiring, supportive individuals who want the best for you. If you are fortunate enough to have such people in your life, always express your gratitude to them.

Whether it is a thing or a person, only
after losing them do we come to know
about their importance.

When love knocks on only one friend's heart, the friendship between a boy and a girl becomes extremely sensitive.

Instead of looking for happiness in others, learn to love and respect yourself more because there is no guarantee that other people will always be good to you.

Even though endings are difficult, there are circumstances when there is no other way to shield ourselves from toxicity.

Like kite flying, love likewise
requires the efforts of two individuals.

There is more peace in telling the truth than
in telling a lie.

We humans have a tendency to take nature for granted, but it always gives us all we need to exist in this world without asking anything in return.

The moon and stars are only visible in the night sky. Similar to this, there are times when we must learn certain things in the dark that we cannot learn in the light.

32

A true friend appreciates you and uplifts your spirit rather than tearing you down.

Don't worry if you are going down in your life, you can rise up again by having faith in yourself.

Do praise people, but carefully,
because excessive praise creates
arrogance in some people, and very
little praise breaks people's morale.

It is very important to make time for each other in relationships because without it, relationships wither just like plants do when they don't receive water on time.

In the journey of life, never lose those

who always want the best for you.

In relationships, sincerity is something I value a lot, but most people nowadays have no idea what it is.

In life, we come across a variety of people. While some bring forth our greatest qualities, others bring out our more caliginous traits.

Keep your distance from people who don't appreciate your presence in their lives and always take you for granted. Sooner or later, you will realise you are more at peace without them in your life.

While making friends, focus on quality, not quantity, to gain real friends in your life.

When things are tough, a loving hug and the

support of our loved ones

can do wonders.

Men must not be the only ones to
make women feel special; women
must also make an effort to make
men feel special.

Even if I'm not perfect, I am conscious that my imperfections are beautiful too and do not make me less than anyone else.

A broken heart knows and
understands the pain of other
broken hearts.

45

Don't take criticism on social media
seriously, and have confidence
in yourself.

You deserve consistent love, not inconsistent love, where a person's love and care for you change according to their mood and needs.

Some people bother other people just for their own entertainment and also purposely try to make them angry. Keep your distance from such people and avoid becoming a source of entertainment for them.

The war between heart and mind is a
very common and tough one.

If you are hurt, then give yourself time to heal, as healing needs time and patience.

Love your people every day, not just on one day. However, it's also okay if you express your love a little bit more on some special days.

Detaching yourself from the people who

were the reason for your pain, tears, and

sadness is not selfish. It is also a part

of self-care.

Always stand up for yourself; never rely on others. You can confidently fight your own struggle alone.

POEMS

Mend your broken heart

The sun is shining brightly in the sky.

The flowers are dancing in the garden.

The grass is becoming greener in the rain.

But the wind is whispering in my ears.

Come on, what are you waiting for?

Let's mend your broken heart and let it fly.

Nights

I paint my nights with happy lies

combined with the camaraderie of fireflies,

The fresh dreams give me happiness

and a hope to vanquish my unhappiness.

Embrace the challenges

A part of me is holding back tears

I'm ready now to face all my fears,

The past tears are like my precious pearls

Always embrace the challenges, you strong girls.

Route to success

The route to success is

 not going to be easy

The speed bumps are

driving me crazy,

I am ready for ups and downs

while chasing my dream

I can do it. That will be my

new confident scream,

One day, I know that

everything will be alright

My own hope will soon

lead me towards soothing light.

Beauty

Beauty is upon you and your perceptions

Different people have different definitions,

Some people find beauty only in perfection

While some also see beauty in imperfection,

For me, beauty is not just the outer appearance

It's also about seeing someone's inner appearance.

Mountains and Beaches

Mountains and beaches

make me delighted, and the

magical peace that I experience

makes me curious to know the

mystery behind nature's

mind-blowing calmness to my

mind and soul for erasing sadness.

Appreciate

Fishes are not crying

about the need for wings

Roses are happy, even

with painful thorns

The sky is joyful with

clouds that want rain

The land is hoping for

many more plants and trees

The sea and oceans are

peaceful, even with waves

Tiny stars are not envious

of such a lovely big moon

And I'm wondering why

we are not like them

We always complain about

what we don't have

Instead of complaining,

start appreciating what you have.

Two gardeners

I used to be a seed

The two gardeners

raised me with their

water of love and care,

protected and supported

me from the strong winds

and instilled the confidence

by standing next to me, even

after growing into a tree.

Happiness

You transformed into a different

person, like a different season,

And I don't know why, as you

didn't tell me the reason.

But I'm happy without you as

my peace is now with me,

I have learned that I can find

happiness only in me.

Strange and Cold

He never gave her the

same kind of love and

support that she gave

to him wholeheartedly,

She is not there for him

anymore, he is wondering

why her behaviour has

changed into something

so strange and so cold.

Love

Love is a growing garland,

Together, we will water it

Decorate it with affection

Tie it with a thread of trust.

Be closer to me always, my dear

One garland is enough for us,

We will protect it from evil hands

Just stay with me till the very end.

Ignorance

Ignorance, we can't say,

is bliss every time,

It's not possible to ignore

some things all the time.

Yes, some situations

demand ignorance,

But, some situations are

ruined by ignorance.

Someone's ignorance makes

us feel like a sharp knife,

It hurts a lot when loved ones

gift you this in your life.

A Rose and the Thorn

I was like an elegant rose

He was an enchanting thorn,

Though we were different

Deep love grew between us,

I thought that love would

last for ever, but I was wrong.

Flowers

Flowers bloom in the spring as a reminder that no matter how pleasant or unpleasant the other seasons are, there will always be one season that will undoubtedly add colour and fragrance in our life.

Pages of Life

Some pages of my life are

filled with so many riddles,

I've been trying really hard to

find all of their answers.

I don't know in which direction

my destiny is moving,

According to God's plan,

everything is surely happening.

One day, sure, I'll get the answers

 to my questions,

Till then, I'm embracing

everything without taking tensions.

A Kite

People will try to

bring you down

while you fly like

a kite in the sky,

Have faith in your

potential to soar

even higher into

the beautiful sky.

Raindrop

Raincoats and umbrellas

shield people from me,

Most toddlers like to dance

 joyfully all the time with me.

I'm a raindrop ,

Sometimes I pour from the clouds,

Sometimes you can see me in

people's joyful or saddened eyes.

It's okay

It's okay to be silent when…..

You really don't want to talk.

Your heart is trying to heal wounds.

You are too happy or sad.

Your people hurt you and ignore you.

You are not ready for something.

Your thoughts are struggling in your mind.

You are confused about what's going on.

Your goals are not going according to plan.

You know that sometimes it's necessary.

Your soul wants to enjoy solitude.

You are searching for yourself.

The old songs

The old songs always capture

my heart with their enchanting

lyrics and soulful lovely music,

Their soothing music creates a

peaceful atmosphere and adds

a touch of fascinating magic,

Listening to them while travelling

by car brings back my old memories

and always makes me feel nostalgic.

Broken crayons

Broken crayons in

my bag are broken,

yet they are content

that I used them to

add colour to my life,

All the crayons are dancing

joyfully and smiling after

witnessing their gorgeous

hues on my glad soul,

Together with their lighter and

79

darker tones, crayons of various

colours, each of which stands for

a particular feeling, promised never

to desert me for more exciting life journeys.

You

You once told me you would be

my umbrella when it rains and

any drops of water try to touch me,

You'll serve as my warm coat

in the winter when I get shivers

due to the cold,

You'll act as my sunblock during

the summer to shield me from

sun's rays,

You'll be my springtime blossom to

cheer me up, and you'll love me the

most in the autumn to lift my spirits,

You once told me all this when you

abruptly appeared in my dream one

night.

A new hope

The rain is falling

from the blue sky,

Tears are falling from

her beautiful eyes.

Everyone is missing

the warm sunlight,

She is missing the

tranquilly at twilight.

The rainbow colours

will soon be visible,

Her dark thoughts

will become invisible.

A new day will bring

peaceful light into life,

A new hope will add

happiness to her life.

Self-Love

I loved you a little more

than I loved myself,

This is what I did wrong to myself.

I ignored and forgot

about the self-love,

While pouring into you all

my true and sincere love.

I remember the mistake of

ignoring my dreams for you,

Now I will love my dreams

first before loving you.

While loving you, I became

 the withered flower,

After loving myself, I'll again

transform into a fresh flower.

The boat of feelings

In the boat

of feelings

you and I were

both travelling,

We held each

other's hands

firmly to survive

the storm of issues

that rocked our boat,

We realised later

that we were in

the ocean of love,

where we must

learn to swim.

Little moments

Beautiful little

moments are

often taken

for granted,

But after some

years, we feel

that these were

the moments

we wanted,

The rising sun,

the scent of a

flower, the buzz

of bees, or the

chirping of birds,

The tranquilly in

these moments

is impossible to

describe in words.

People

Surround yourself with people who

support you in achieving your goals,

Observe who guides you unconditionally

to see a better version of yourself.

The real gems always get joy from

supporting you and seeing your success,

The fake ones can't see you in a

place while making some progress.

It doesn't matter whether the support

is from strangers or known people,

The only thing that matters is who

puts effort into building your confidence.

People who genuinely care for you are

worthy of keeping close to your heart,

When someone tries to put you down,

make them remember where the door is.

The path of life

I'm travelling on

the path of life,

Sometimes it feels like

walking on a knife.

I don't know anything

about my destination,

Just enjoying every direction

without hesitation.

Some roads on my way give

off the vibe of happiness,

Some just test me by creating

bumps of sadness.

I'll travel and face everything

with a big smile,

No storm can stop me, nor

can it make me fragile.

Vibha is an Indian writer who originally belongs to Delhi, India. She has done B.Com. from Jabalpur, Madhya Pradesh, and a Diploma in Interior Designing from Kolkata, West Bengal. She also worked for a few months at an architectural firm in Delhi. She likes doing creative work and believes that writing also needs creativity. Apart from writing, she also loves reading, art, crafts, and photography.